MW01071610

Winter Sharp with Apples

Also by Annette Sisson

Small Fish in High Branches
A Casting Off (chapbook)

Winter Sharp with Apples

Annette Sisson

Terrapin Books

© 2024 by Annette Sisson
Printed in the United States of America.
All rights reserved.
No part of this book may be reproduced in any manner,
except for brief quotations embodied in critical articles
or reviews.

Terrapin Books
4 Midvale Avenue
West Caldwell, NJ 07006

www.terrapinbooks.com

ISBN: 978-1-947896-75-8
Library of Congress Control Number: 2024941240

First Edition

Cover art: David Ribar
Bodhi, 18" x 12"
digital image

Cover design: Diane Lockward

for Jimmy
again, and always

Contents

III. Woodlanders

IV. Epilogue

"The pleasures of heaven are with me, and the pains of hell
    are with me.
The first I graft and increase upon myself. The latter I translate
    into a new tongue."
                    —Walt Whitman, *Leaves of Grass* (1855)

"The stroke of genius from early farmers was to realize they
could bypass the sexual dance and produce plants . . .
without seeds. Take a small cutting from a mature apple
tree, graft it onto mature rootstock, and it'll produce perfectly
identical apples."
            —Daniel Stone, *The Food Explorer: The True Adventures
            of the Globe-Trotting Botanist Who Transformed What
            America Eats* (2018)

Origin Story

In the end, we'll all become stories.
        —Margaret Atwood, *Moral Disorder and Other Stories*

I lie on a frayed quilt in a back acre,

sweep my eyes across the dusky glass:

jeweled studs of stars, nebulas in haze—

metal stippling on a black satin canvas.

My mind fastens on the belly of this silver river,

unreels, aches to touch life's nucleus.

Galaxies of cells spiral, cobalt and amber

whirl into green. To still the swirl, I focus

on the febrile moon, sense its contours of despair,

ecstasy: kernel of being // seed of death—

twin chambers of a cracked walnut, a pair

of fibrous lungs teetering on the edge of breath.

I. Unburying the Roots

Nature Almost Holds Us

On a grainy black and white video
the mandible of my grandson's large skull
opens, closes—a flapping gate
inside a storm of amniotic fluid.

> *Autumn's rainless weeks cannot*
> *dissuade sweet gum from its scarlet frippery—*
> *leaves blaze and flap in morning*
> *air chilly as well water.*

The surgeon chisels a tiny hole
in my father's good eye, fashions
a thin flap to cover the pit—
a pot of churning liquid, lid
placed askew, tension releases.

> *Night's cloudy tarp, curve*
> *of thin light—too little to see*
> *the bird's angle of flight, only*
> *the whoosh and flap above my head—*
> *thrust of air, beats recede.*

In Fort Myers my son hangs
shutters on his condo, flap hinges
screwed to wood face, sturdy
latches. Hurricane Ian submerges
Sanibel, hoists its load to the mainland.

A hairy woodpecker drills the birdhouse
wall. In the garden weeds flourish
in drought, creeping thyme and salvia
wither. Digger bees climb
from a dusty tunnel, bustle and flap.

My father orders me to leave his house—
Get out! Go home! I don't want you
here!—the fight in his voice simmering
for months. The word *flap* lodges
in my ear, its rough-hewn percussion—
f and *p* rasp the silence raw.

Muscle Memory

I.

The late-night train
      blares, wheels squeal
on iron, like the season
      of my mother's first cancer.
I was eight, studying
      the grim jaws of muted
grown-ups. A young boy,
      you too worried, creasing
baseball cards while your parents
      smoked and smoked, kitchen
walls brown with nicotine.

II.

We lug our stunted childhoods
      like rusted spikes. Chains
and mauls. We recoil from flat cars,
      covered hoppers, runaways—
fold into time, into pattern,
      rhythm, the howl of engines,
clang of push and pull.
      There is no forswearing
of air blast and signal,
      of memory, the wailing movement
of diesel, piston, freight.

Seeds

*In one weekend alone, more than 80 babies were born in
bomb shelters in Kyiv.*
　　　　　　　—Mathias Bölinger, March 13, 2022

Already a million people have fallen
off the edge of their rickety lives,
landed on trains and vans, carried
away from the walls that held them,
through the silhouettes of hills outside Kyiv
where branches stir the settling fog.

Behind a fence a woman thrusts
words at a reporter: *I would kill him
with my own bare hands.* Later
a thirteen-year-old girl implores:
*It has to stop—pregnant women
underground giving birth.* In tunnels
and basements, infants wait for their first
breaths—spring seeds, already buried,
pressed into dirt by a bloody thumb.

Laid Bare

Empty air between the basement slab

and scattered gravel three feet
below—erosion unsettling brick,

mortar, uprights, trusses. We stared,

pictured bones, cartilage,
femurs, pelvises laid bare.

We had traipsed across that cement

a million times to slide open
the heavy door, watch our daughter

scale the monkey bars, help her

scrub the golden retriever. Workmen
pummeled the concrete, cleared away

the jagged pieces. We peered into the pile

of fresh rocks, new floor mixing,
then poured, reinforced, sealed against

rivers of grief. Still, I know

the shock of a hole so immense
it swallows the body. Across the ocean

my daughter sends a text. She's fainted

on the bathroom tile of a Madrid bistro—
cracked ceramic, vomit, not sure

how long she was out. Alone,

woozy, she types, *I don't know what
to do.* Or her call from a Nashville clinic—

doctor, needle biopsy, she needs us

to bring her home. I fall through
these moments, watch my body

sink, a vacant sac flattened—

the joists of a house folding in,
jolt of air filling the cavities,

whispers in the gaps between ribs.

Turf

[grass is] a shag rug
laid over the scuffed floors of history.
  —Danusha Laméris, "The Grass," *Bonfire Opera*

My daughter nudges the praying mantis
marooned high on the storefront window,
its body a tapered spear of celery.

Below—cliffs of glass, rivers
of cement, prairies of asphalt. She rifles
through her bag, pulls out a bank

deposit slip, slides it under the mantis,
the sagging paper on the checkbook,
glides away mindful as a bride.

When she reports the tiny corner
of green she found behind Target, I nod,
tell her a story—the iniquities of grass.

Dazzled by Europe's fussy lawns
the Founding Fathers imported carpets
of emerald: Monticello, Mount Vernon,

golf courses green as cash,
diamond-cut suburbs, the decadence
of irrigation. Grass, an invasive, snuffs

out weeds and wildflowers, then pollen,
bees, flies—the feasts of predator
insects. Perhaps this history of lawns

is redeemed by its sweet blades, *fibers*
from the hair of the dead. But our loves,
strewn about us in acres of green, might have

become mantises, feeding on pollinators,
cavorting on dappled rugs of meadow,
part bluestar, part dandelion.

An Ecology of Shells

Broadkill Beach, Delaware

I.

My mother lived in landlocked states,
leery of oceans, barely a swimmer.
Yet her bathroom was heaped with shells,
some purchased at home décor
stores, others bestowed by friends.
I photographed my toddler seated
in clover, wearing a diaper. My mother
limned this picture on canvas, finished it
in oils but set him in the ocean's surf.
She hung the painting low, piled
the bathtub's rim with polished husks
that once held sea creatures,
accented now by pastel bath soaps—
oysters, starfish, graceful spirals of whelks.

II.

Horseshoe crabs clutter the evening
shore. The hollow shells might have
detached to make way for larger coverings.
The ones with carcasses must have mated,
buried the eggs, lingered on the beach
too long. Slipper shells once
bearing snails festoon the crabs'

dark helmets, crustaceans like gemstones.
Did the snails that mounted these rounded
ships to breed outlast their triumph?
As their pilot trundled to shore, clawing
the sand embankment, could they know
this striving to copulate would be the end?

III.

Birds cluster at the salt marsh.
Boat-tailed grackles buzz and rattle.
Sandpipers pluck insects from the shallows.
Snowy egrets jostle toward a bed
of fiddler crabs at the water's edge.
Unfazed, the males sidle, entice
females, brandish and tap their gleaming
major claws, circadian rhythms
calibrated to the ebb and flow of ocean tide.

IV.

A man drives a pickup onto the beach,
loads horseshoe crabs into the bed
until shells mound above the tailgate.
An old woman saunters along
the dunes, asks him why so many.
*I sell them for fish bait, like my father
always did.* She alludes to breeding

season, questions the size of his haul.
He stops work, slams the cab's
door, seals the window tight as a clam.

V.

The girl appears in front of my bench
on the dock—a teenager, autistic.
Open your hands, she commands.
I cup them under her fist, wary of muck
and slime. She waits, face blank
as sand until our hands line up,
nods, drops a small gray shell,
scurries off, returns with a second,
iridescent, places it in my palm
without touching my skin. She fades
into collage—floppy hats, towels,
tackle boxes, sinuous mounds of water.

Reverie

I.

I take my young son to the zoo, New Year's Eve, buttoned
against the cold. As we leave the Siberian, I ask him, *Can
this one kill you?* I know it can — toddlers, adults, no matter —
but does he? Will knowing keep him alive? We approach the
Reptile House, array of camouflage like the Caneback I once
nearly stepped on. Behind glass, rattlers wind among rocks,
rivulets of leathered air; my son inhales, caught in the thrall
of scales.

II.

That night, a nightmare: a giant
snapping turtle in the foyer

threatens the toddler, beak grazing
his shins, my lunge too late.

III.

My mother dispenses news of her brother's cancer: He calls
her crying, lost in his own house. Her family fades away, a
season of dying — a cousin killed in a house fire, her sister
suicidal, her mother wasted, slipping away while faith
healers pray. My mother sketches the table decked with the

depression ware her brother collected, strokes the pale dress
he gave her forty years ago.

IV.

After my uncle's burial, my son will chase the lanky white
kitten through my mother's kitchen, corral the cat, order it to
freeze, to remain in his compass. My mother will beckon
him to the stairwell closet, to her newest painting still
unframed: the kitten, immutable, perched before a cut-glass
vase of roses, lavender and burnished orange—the bouquet
she placed on her brother's bedside table the last time.

V.

First hours of the new year
mirror a black-sheened sky.

My son puffs small regular
breaths. I reach for a nightgown,

burrow into dream, turtles hulking
so slow I think I might catch them.

Threadbare

Like milk pouring from a glass
bottle, the mourning dove's

velvet coo summons
my childhood in a mellow town

still tying off
its long seam of sleep.

Bedroom windows open
to the tang of cut grass,

tender violets, white-
tufted clover. Bumblebees

throb, thorns bristle
in sidewalk cracks

but I don't heed their stings
or stabs. In a later house

on three acres of field
meted out in fabric swatches,

we snap annual photos
beside the boulder in the backyard,

my brother tends his first
monarch chrysalis, my mother's

second cancer shrouds
the windowpanes of my room.

When I add *morning dove*
to our list of bird sightings,

Mom apprises me of the missing *u*.
I hear its muffled call—

not velvet, but thread unraveling.

What the Scan Doesn't Show

The CT scan rewrites the story of her broken
shoulder. A heart attack knocked her off
the couch, her fractured scapula
collateral damage, a second
layer of dominoes
falling.

It doesn't expose her motives, why she had
her teeth removed, refused the plan
for implants, hides away in her
cluttered den, cancels lawn
care, exterminators,
housekeeper.

It doesn't show the conflicts she frets over—her rituals
of checking: investment accounts, weather in
Birmingham, Jackson, Asheville (the cities
where her children live), websites of
their employment. She prefers to
browse, not to be family.
A scan cannot
pinpoint
why.

Keeping Sunrise

4:30 a.m. Your finger pecked, rapid and staccato,
on my bedroom window. Already dressed, I met

you by the side door of the garage. We pushed
bikes through driveway gravel, large and loose

as Tinker Toy spools, tires too thin for anything
but blacktop. Headlights, reflectors, white sweatshirts,

we rode the night raw, rubber humming, stars
suspended, waiting for early light to blanch

out their faces. We ditched our wheels in a ravine
that fell away from the railroad tracks, traipsed

across ties and trestle to a rocky stretch
where the tree line yawned. We settled in for sunrise,

shivered in June's early nip. Though we knew
the train wouldn't barrel through till 8:00 a.m.,

we imagined stray engines muscling toward us,
plotted scenarios of grim escape—bruises,

fractures—then lapsed into our usual banter:
Gollum's ring, planetary orbits, Monty

Python's *Spam*, Bach's intricate fingerings.
We hushed as the peach aura singed the air,

applauded the sun, the climb from our snug covers,
the pancakes your mother, in another hour, would shovel

onto our plates. We knew too that we clapped
for our gritty hopes, blooms of warm breath,

kiss of distant stars. This was the script,
our timing perfect. We basked in each streak

of colored light, refracted by cloud and mist.
Later we devised another script, braided

our plot strands tight, tweaked the hours
down to the last thread—still the timing

slipped. This was the one we couldn't finish.
Day that wouldn't break.

M. Shelley's Interrogation

For while I destroyed his hopes, I did not satisfy my own desires.
—Monster, *Frankenstein*

If computers expunge humanity,
would their pulsing motherboards
replicate human flaws?

Drones with nervous tics
scratching themselves in public,
clumps of automatons averting

their gaze? Cluttered microchips
multiplying data, hoarding
fragments of cursive? Would

robots dab watercolor light
onto rough press paper, or glide
a bow, suffer the trembling

strings to mourn? Could
the warbler's chipped trill,
the moon-white orchid

stir their sensors, the Luna's
lobed wing brush
mystery into code? And if

they chose a god to humble them,
might they pray to their creators'
ashes? Would we kindle

ourselves, put on the Godhead,
breathe in translucence—
claim this progeny our own?

On the Brink

I remember your voice, how it soared
         and dipped. You perched on the chair as if

    touching its back might shatter something—
         the wooden slats, or your shoulder.

The trip had changed you—the native people,
     their lives so close to the earth.

    Your words faltered, spilled. You retrieved them,
       called this feeling *the baobab tree*—

you wanted to turn the world with your hands.
     A month later you hiked to a tower,

    scaled the scaffolding, hurled yourself off.
       What ghost broke you? How

did the brain unfasten? Muddy snow,
     twilight, your body there, beside

    the steel truss—mist descends,
       thins under a slivered moon.

Portrait of My Father's Glaucoma

My father pushes the menu across
  the table, presses me to order
his breakfast. He echoes *over easy*
  to the waiter, fumbles for ketchup,
creamer. Egg yolks trickle from fork
  to jacket. I retrieve his napkin, dab
at the spots. Rising to leave, he clenches
  my sleeve. I steer him around potholes,
survey the sky, a worn gray
  tarpaulin: blotches mingle, coagulate—
conifers sweep the morning dry.
  He edges to the car's open door.
Wind catches a flock of turkey
  vultures—solemn crosses, blur.

Duende

How can I say that a bay mare
calls me, her umber eye latched
to mine; that the mourning doves

keening outside my window etch
their lament on the blade of my sternum;
that the terrier's chin on my knee,

rump nuzzling my bare feet—
dark jar of sangria, hint
of dregs in the first sip? In May's

fleshy tendrils I see claws
of drought, autumn's flush of decay,
convulsions of ice, a sepia winter

drudging beneath hollow stalks.
Every day my heart contracts,
expands, valves swooshing—

every day its thud echoes
heavy in my belly. Among hallowed bones,
I hearken to the bees' intrepid whir,

say: *nectar, wing, wax, elixir.*

Under a White Moon

A daughter, now eighty-two, spends
a decade grubbing in dirt, unburying

the transplanted roots of her life.

She returns to this place, searches for roses—
Granada War Relocation Center,

rocky, once covered with chain-link,

barbed wire, seven thousand
Japanese Americans fenced away

like nightshade. After Pearl Harbor,

her mother took a cutting from her lost
grandparents' rosebush, stashed it

into a *satcheru*, under a slim volume

of Bashō, a hand mirror inlaid
with mother of pearl—tokens to fuel

dreams of pagodas, lotus blossoms imperial

as kabuki. At the camp the mother waited
for the moon's white shine, planted

the shoot while the guards slept—wormed

her way out of the hammock to a patch
of land with thicker soil, dug the hole

with a borrowed spoon and pearl handle.

Eight decades later the daughter
finds one pink bloom, a bud

on a small bramble, petals drawn

tight as a pill bug—she remembers
the dusty corners of the wire enclosure,

sees her mother's hands grafting roses,

hears her whisper to the stems' nodes:
It's the roots that save; push them deep.

II. Limbs Propagate in the Split

Her Offering

I.

One by one before they
ripened in my front yard,

the skins split, coral
flesh of cantaloupe gaping.
I suspected raccoon, opossum,

deer, the heat—certainly not
the Eastern box turtle

plodding through shadowed vines,
snug under its stenciled carapace,
saffron-eyed among chiseled

rinds, spilled seeds,
the raw viscera of loss.

II.

My mother compiled a list
of marriage partners for my father.
For after she passed. My parents

recited the litany of candidates
over and over, revising,

parsing pros and cons
until my mother paused,
too frail to carry on.

    III.

Here in this garden, honeyed
with carnage, I see at last

my mother's kindness, how
she offered herself, the fruit
of her overripe body, untangled

the withering vine of her illness,
fashioned him a sequel,

a shell like a shield etched
with widows' names. Perhaps
she hoped one would slip

the cover off, crack
open the hull of him,

gather the scattered kernels,
salvage a cantaloupe, roughly
inscribed, before summer's end.

Caney Fork

Autumn crisps the tapering light,
      oak pulls on its auburn duster.
We drive beside the river to the steep
      orchard where apple trees climb
the furrowed ridge. In fall we recall
      how the tang of applesauce, native
and ardent as old marriage, staves off
      winter's crisis of ice. En route
we wonder: Will the bent woman
      still be there? Or will she have joined
the earth somewhere between hollow and hill?

You find the crack in the dell, nose
      our car down the dirt drive.
Through the shack's murky window,
      we see her dark form move.
She opens the unsprung door,
      offers her creaky smile; we hunch
inside, hair dusting the low
      lintel, breathe in apples,
ask for Mullins—*Rusty Coats*,
      she mumbles, loads them into bushel
baskets; we hand her folded cash,
      lug the haul to the trunk, nod,
a shadow waving, pull away.

Down the road the Caney Fork.

You cut the engine. I choose to wait
on the bank, you follow the cascades, navigate
        the jagged rocks halfway across.
I watch a heron stalk, dive,
        swallow a small bream. The bird
ruptures the air as it rises, marks
        time in high breeze, finds
the tree line's gap, disappears
        over the bluff. I blink, scan
for your silhouette, framed in a plot of sun
        against cliffs where river widens, sky
opens. You are a shade dancing
        in light, a paper figure flitting
on wire. I picture the wire thickening
        to rope, me pulling your body,
hand over hand, back to shore.

The retreating beats of the bird's
        wings echo. I think of the apple
woman, dilapidated shed, pungent
        harvest—the honeyed zest of my mother's
apple tart, her ashes strewn
        under a broad maple last January.
I want to hear you breathe,
        slide my fingers through your arms,
lock them between the shoulder blades.
        Distance and time, a heron's flight—
its absence, perhaps its return. I want
        to glide across that stretch of miles
back to the grizzled woman sorting

     fruit, to catch her rusty voice,
see her wave us off again,
     the sleeves of her blowsy jacket fanning
wind, a winter sharp with apples.

Marriage at Ten Years, 1963

In long strokes, almost photographic,
a meadow ripples with blooms, bits
of sunlit colored glass. A path
divides the field, leads to a clapboard

house with large windows, tall
plaster walls, a broad front porch
where a woman lingers, arms
wrapped around a carved white post,

her skin bright as the paint, thick
brown hair in waves. A calico cat
rubs against her shins, noses
her toe. Like a Wyeth but more

color, a Hopper with softer lines.
My young mother at twenty-eight
treasures this image, a postcard a friend
sent from New York City, keeps it

in the nightstand beside the double bed
she shares with her husband. She studies the life
in the painting—the enameled newel, almondy
sedge, the breeze, glints of color

swaying, lanky stalks. She smooths
morning into afternoon, wonders how
to set a table as luscious as the garden
she sketches in her notebook—a plot of hollyhocks,

four-o'clocks she'd like to plant in spring.
For now the yard is patchy, the porch
narrow, the cat and kits she took
to raise deserted on a country road.

She frets about rent, the cost of running
a household. Inside, a throw pillow
balances on the sofa back, conceals
splintered plaster gouged by the Hawkeye

camera she lobbed at him for signing up
to bowl a third night, for his relief,
stranding her at home with a toddler and baby.
She consults the postcard, notes how

the woman in the painting waits alone—
turns to her sketchpad, pictures the garden
she'll dig if the lease is renewed, the wildflower
seeds she'll scatter in the front yard.

Clutch

Nothing was automatic. Not
    my mother's grip slipping
on my skin, nor her 1973
    Dodge Dart—stubborn
three-speed, stiff wheels,
    no power steering,
the color of a clingstone peach.
    For spring graduation she stitched
a dorm quilt, helped me choose
    an electric typewriter—even
showed me how to drive
    the Dart: shift the gears,
guide the clutch, accelerate,
    swell into forward glide.
But our summer sputtered and lurched—
    Mom hounding me to stay
home, me swiping
    keys from her zippered purse,
screeching out of the driveway.

    After Labor Day we stood on hot
pavement, limestone dormitory
    looming, hours of unloading
boxes, tangled hangers,
    bedmaking—the room's cement
blocks sweating. We shuffled
    to the end of the path, afternoon

heat rolling into thunder.

      I couldn't shake off the rain,
lift my feet to go inside.

      I watched as my mother scudded
through puddles, clicked the Dart's

      ignition, placed one hand
on the wheel, the other on the rearview

      mirror, adjusting. Clouds
churned and hovered. She switched

      the wipers on, pressed
the gas, released the clutch.

Late

My mother presses the vein
on the top of her hand, asks

if I regret the abortion.
Her voice lingers, eyes

fixed on the kitchen window.
I stir the soup again,

replace the stainless lid,
gnaw the membrane inside my lip.

Many years ago
I heard her breath clutch—

silence on the phone line
as she pictured me splayed

on a bare table, the trickle
of blood. For thirty years

she hadn't asked. Nursed
this ghost, banded it in certainty.

Mom, I was never pregnant.
My period finally came.

She releases the fusty air
from her chest, lays down

the wraith of raw belief
she's carried like a blade.

First Coffee

In the kitchen, housecoat barely
tied, she waits for water
to boil. First coffee

of her sixty-sixth year.
Time drifts, dust
coils in shafts of light.

At six months her grandson
squeals, scoots himself
across the floor. She wonders

if her next car will pass
to him, a teen, as she
barters for rides—doctor,

pharmacy, grocery store—
her sons, fifty by then,
one bald as a newborn,

the other silver-gray.
Coffee filtered, she watches
the splotch of milk expand,

fade, sips gently
to steady the clock in her head —
ponders how long

her shoulders will swivel, flex
to stroke the baby's back
as he slides into swales of sleep.

Octopus

In early-hour half-light, he launches
    the thirty-foot trawler, ten hours
of bending, dragging, pulls a hard
    living from Falmouth Bay, deep
coves, ragged map of tunnels,
    water so clear the algae's
pile can be gauged from the cliff: thin
    lime, emerald, evergreen velour.

Rubberized pants circle his waist,
    cinched in back, straps over scrappy
shoulders, knife tucked into loop.
    He leans over new catch
in stacked crates, blankets the open
    top with a towel. Plastic containers
winch, swing boat to air, ocean
    tumbling through the holes. And then:

Tentacles flail softly from the middle
    carton's wall. Some shorter,
some long, smooth, tapered,
    white, pink edges. Rows
of suckers ripple as the sleek flesh
    twists. The small crowd awaiting
a ferryboat is riveted. Is this mollusk
    reaching for one more hold?

How can agile ropes of muscle
    be so opaline, so lush? Why
wrench this creature from its den? I recoil
    from fisherman, dock, turn to sea—

turquoise surging beneath gusts of somber
    sky. Beside the octopus, I dive
into silver-black caverns, slice
     the dark, squeeze into eelgrass, crevice,
       flinch beside knots of wafting net.

First Morning, 2023

In the Blue Ridge mountains
granite swells its barrel
chest along the roadside.

Strands of clouds sheath
valleys, swallow trees
up to their crowns.

Blue-gray hills convene
in haze, and patches of bare
brush congregate on nearby

slopes, ringed in white
light. Already morning
kindles spent embers,

marrow of bone and earth.

Our Hands

Three months after you die, recede
into silver mist, a grandchild will be born.

With fingertips that once grazed your cheek,
I will touch this baby—and he will be yours.

I will cradle him in our hands, picture
how you would swaddle his body, lose myself

in your strokes. Hunched to my chest, he will drift
to the sound of your blood sluicing. When he wakes,

I will whisper how your gray hair rustles
on the shoulder of your sky-blue nightgown,

circle him high overhead, a small plane,
raise him through the veil, arms wide, skimming.

Galloping in Darkness

He claims the basement bedroom of his parents'
      three-story, rolls the walls in black,
inks the shallow ceiling. A three-dimensioned
      midnight to slip into. Inside this box

he piles equestrian medals, math
      awards, golden mitts crowned
with baseballs, to stow in the attic, far
      from his mother's polishing cloth, his father's

swagger and framed degrees. At sixteen
      he loathes the weight of trophies—coins
to feed the machine of his parents' need.
      He wonders what life will be, doesn't

see his shoulders broadening. His fingernail
      traces the floor tile's grout
as if it mapped the future. In the windowless
      room he longs for night air,

heads outside, past the orchard,
      lifts the barn's latch, the saddle.
Boots in stirrups, twitch of mane,
      animal pulse—he turns into galloping

wind, a bitter tearing through dark,

       blind to snags, low branches.

He hunches into the horse's neck, coursing

       toward flecks of dawn, panting for light.

Blue Spruce

A somber autumn, season of drought
and divorce. I read about cleft grafting,
wonder how limbs propagate in the split.

You arrive in your silver Chevy pickup,
bring a Colorado spruce for my blue-
eyed son, shoulder it inside,

clip the low sprigs, shimmy
trunk into metal, rotate, lock it
down. I had shunned Christmas,

the shuffling through trim, boxes
of painted fragments, too sharp,
too heavy to open. You splice

strands, weave spangled light
into branches, needles soft. The tree
settles, stretches for tinsel and beads.

Maybe a braided nest of eggs,
sky-blue, to roost in an elbow's bend.

Lava

Your childhood stories rehashed a single
narrative arc: *happiness, hot lava, victory.*
When your father left, you revised the plot:

All ended with his move to a house on our block.
The splintered years heaped in piles, dry
twigs on an angry brushfire. Your silence simmered,

smoldered, earth's veins, the igneous core—
a fevered gash, scalding silicon, sulfur,
magma. Red dust charged the air,

a striated sun. Then lichens and ferns
unfurled, cracked crust into particles of soil—
old stories new closure. Now your words

are water, smooth and cool as glass, your voice
sea spray, your longing a river of pebbles,
inlets of blue islands, troves of ash.

Transfiguration

Holy Island of Lindisfarne

This small earth, the tide's salt-edged tongues, damp licking. Breath eddies, swells the sponge of lungs, lobes suspended amid sky and sea, exhaling, exhaling. Gust gathers, sweeps through the priory ruins, presses sheaves of basalt, wrenches cord grass and bogbean—the chest-hinge opens. Blood thumps. Gale surges, crests, pummels laps of sand. Ancient monks murmur, figments in spray. Slick, mercurial bodies, molded heads—grey seals bob in surf; they lumber to shore, clamber onto rock, keep vigil, quiet as gospel on calfskin.

Flight Season

after "Gulf Coast Highway," *by Hooker, Flowers, & Griffith*

I.

Somewhere in Texas a blackbird
    glides across a long
        flat highway. Flocks
of bluebonnets purple beneath
    its shadow as it recedes, a horizon
        of rusting oil wells.
This morning my Dallas cousin
    reports her condition—recurrence
        of cancer, her son suctions
mucous from her lungs. She celebrates
    being home, alive—her voice
        shimmering, cadence and trill
of birdsong. I try to muster
    lyrics for her tune, picture her
        winging into the dark eye of flight.

II.

My children trundle boxes
    to apartments, babies to homes
        in distant cities. I visit,
stretch the rounded hours
    thin and long, lift
        the toddler's hand to trace

my cheekbone, jawline, then
    her own. At bath time I towel
        water from her skin, repeat:
bath, lake, river, rain.
    That night I crouch in the shower,
        my lower back wrenched.
My husband rushes upstairs,
    reports blackbirds cluttering
        the tops of the Japanese maples.
The day creases like paper—
    angular birds with folded
        wings, forked tails.

III.

My father's eyes wither
    like cut blossoms. Chickadees
        pluck seeds from the neighbor's
feeder, my father blind
    to their presence. I watch his world,
        his body, shrink—my hands
tending sprightly daylilies,
    digging for kindred roots,
        tubers in soft loam.
At eighty-seven, he wonders
    how many mornings
        he must wake and dress.
Across my cornea blackbirds
    flit like specks of cobweb,
        dart away when I focus.

III. Woodlanders

First Language

A girl of five, she dreams in tongues
of bark and root. She mounts rungs
nailed to a burred trunk, grasps
the greening branch above her head,
wrests her small body up.
Hands, elbows, knees, feet,
she scrambles one fork to the next.

Leaves imbibe light, obscure
her parents' jagged morning, brows
drawn, checkbook splayed open,
the hiss and rasp of brittle tongues.
Harbored among nest and twig,
she idles, drifts, breathes in
ripples of breeze, exhales sky.

Memo to a Fledgling

Bathe with dust in summer, water in winter.
Preen. Keep your speckled feathers spry —

wingtip and scapula to peel back wind.
Notice, casement glass is not the same

as open air. If wing is damaged, retreat
to a scrap of leggy grass. Flatten your body

in a bed of dirt, picture yourself clay.
Dredge for beetle, termite wedged in crevice.

Choose the slouching sunflower other birds spurn.
Examine each seed before piping it down

the black gullet of your dreams. Let it feed
the skylark in you, silver song like rain.

At sixteen, instead of practicing piano,

I drifted through back acres
          to the tree line, wove
                    through dry brush around
a downed sugar maple,
          soft bark spread
                    across clover and nutsedge, sinking
to humus. Fiery leaves
          scattered like light, tongued
                    the bright air. A fallen
pin oak draped the bounding
          creek. I swayed and balanced
                    along its trunk, alighted
in denser shade, untied
          sweatshirt from waist, head
                    and arms into fleece—then straddled
a crumbling elm, grooves
          and knots poking through heavy
                    denim. Sparrow, jay,
cardinal, squirrel, constant
          as the stream wending over
                    and under twig and stone,
thoughtlessly making its way.
          I opened my journal, bent
                    to the page, became acorn,
goldenrod, crow—waves
          of words skimmed paper
                    and breeze. I lifted my eyes—

low sun straight
      ahead, a dark slash
            of limb stenciled silver.
Cows wailed in pastures
      beyond the trees—I heard
            my mother call to me,
one of her last petitions,
      as if she might launch
            into song, dark lament,
flume of water churning.

After a Long Indiana Winter, 1964

My father lost his job in a season
of snowstorms, unable to handle
the roads even with tire chains
on the old yellow Buick. I was five.

When winter thawed, Mom and I planted
a garden behind our rental: salvia,
marigolds, morning glories for a trellis,
bachelor buttons. As we dug the bed,

cleaned out grass and weeds thick
against cement blocks, she instructed me
about seeds, how temperature and rain,
soil and air, work together

to crack them open. She culled the dead
matter, remnants of another tenant—
blossoms and stems spent into dried
straw. Among the withered plants

a small bird, a goldfinch, still,
tangled in spurge and bindweed.
Mom pulled him free, sent me
inside to fetch toilet paper and the empty

kitchen matchbox we'd discarded
that morning. She spread the tissue

across my fleshy palm, placed
the bird on top. We inspected the body,

wings, markings. She helped me roll
the tissue around him, several turns,
lay him in the box which she slid
open. A gold corpse, a winding

sheet, the matchbox she'd reached for
every day to light the gas stove.
We buried him in the garden, leveled
the ground, lined out furrows for our seeds,

pushed them into the soft earth's crust.
All summer we weeded and watered.
Morning glories curled, purple
blooms, eyes shut to noon,

the narrow plot clotted with color—
salvia red as blood, flocks of marigolds.

Adagio

The lily bulbs disintegrate—
infestation and soil fatigue.
Mockingbirds cease to counterfeit
song. It is almost August.

Classroom walls sweat.
Dread churns, settles in
like starlings. I huddle in the hall,
long to skulk away,

slip down the back stairs—
maybe a tall ridge, or
the woods to track the straggling
creeks, crepe myrtle,

to linger over bending fuscia—
small consolations, like
my students' lilac eyes,
flicker of questions, like butterflies.

Unfolding

My daughter hands me
        a fan
                to disperse the swelter
                   of Spain
        black tapered slats
      scarlet roses
              cuts of lattice below
        the spread of blossoms
accordioned like her life
           in Madrid
      where she flutters
                through unlit streets
        scorches her skin
                 under alien sun
     recites conversation scripts
                  alone
dances at a discothèque
     while her phone   coat   purse   all her money
        are taken

Still
        she sculpts the hours
               into alabaster clouds
         fastens them
            to an arch of royal sky

She positions the fan
                    between my thumb
                              and index finger
          tilts my wrist
snaps hers open
                    demonstrates how to stir
                              the sultry afternoon
                    shuffle heat
froth it   like meringue
          how to conjure breath

Daughter, Driving at Night

I slide into bed, turn toward the curtains.

Outside, clear midnight sky,
moon and dippers wheeling across

the galaxy. I begin to drift. A girl

shrieks, frenetic particles of sound,
her voice so piercing it might

have cracked the window. The cry

shivers the air again. I shake
myself, scramble to the front door—

silver dusting the silent walk,

stars' bent ribs of light.
From the screened porch in back

katydids chant, crickets trill,

a tranquil night. Inside, my phone
jars the table—you've driven miles

beyond home, whisper of gas in the tank,

your signal too faint for digital maps,
and you can't tell left from right

without Google. Parked on an unlit shoulder,

you shudder, marvel that your call jostled
me awake. You don't know the quake

of your need had already torn me from the sheets.

Fourth Wall

A young boy studies a cormorant
in a sprawling office lobby, believes
he's found God embodied in bronze.

Mesmerized, he splices each angle,
frames a story, unreels a vision
no one else can see. Thirty

years later he wonders whether
it matters—this gem his mother polishes
like a diamond. He can't bring himself

to take the stone, turn it with his fingers,
examine the facets. If he could,
he might fade into a telescopic lens,

train the thin slice of glass
on a clouded leopard, its ankle bone
rotating as it climbs backwards up

a knobby trunk. Or pivot his scope
to a bayou, trail a lone anhinga
surfacing to feed, snake-like beak

paring the water. What if the wildness
inside him sprang free, nerve
and muscle uncoiled as he stretched for the first

limb, and the next, image flashing
into story—the tale of a gibbon tearing
the air with its high siren howl.

Beyond

Sometimes the hills outside the back door
roil with the stench of skunk.

      Or weasel? Tonight a creature peeps
      in the dark—its faint whistle strengthens

to a small yawp. The dog and I
halt on the sidewalk. Back inside,

      I tip my ear to the open window.
      Not owl. Beyond me. Like last night's

dream. I finally find you, husband,
your face vibrant, hillside of wild

      rudbeckia—eyes cleaved to mine,
      your hand waving me on.

Death is not

the hoot owl   stiff in quiet grass

                the cat   vanished outside
the sliding glass

      a father   spine compressed   coffin
six inches too long

                the doe
plucked away by a coven of vultures

children   their years spooled tight   wasted

                the wood roach   murdered
with impunity

snakes   no more skins to shed

a mother

casket draped with the comforter   she stitched

                even buzzards

Where do they go?

bodies   residue

merge   with soil

molecules

                                    break
   into earthworm

      grass

        tree

What of their glistening threads?

The heave of their leaving?

no wisp of fur   in its curved beak—

death is not   a barred owl

on the forest floor

still

beside   a shagbark

Statistics

The wall along the South Bank bursts with shining
red hearts, all the way from Westminster Bridge
to Lambeth. *Why valentines in July?* we wonder,
push on to the Florence Nightingale Museum.
Inside the low-slung building, Nightingale's fastidious
records, her mastery of statistics, line graphs
of injuries, dysentery, cholera, typhus. Scatter plots
wielded like weapons, to tout antiseptics, make others
see what she saw, bacteria and virus rupturing
soldiers' lives like artillery. Beside the ticket desk
we exit into afternoon drizzle. Threading through
streets, markets, the gardens of St. Thomas Hospital,
past smokers in wheelchairs, revolving fountain,
dahlia, delphinium, we hurry for a close-up of the wall.
There, across from Parliament, there, in Big Ben's
sightlines, it curves out of view, every inch laden
with hearts except for a bronze plaque: *The National
Covid Memorial Wall*. 228,000 small markers
in concrete. Down the sidewalk a young woman
extends her hand above her head, scrawls with a black
Sharpie. Endless epitaphs, names—and the mourners,
still here, on this path, facing the structure, bearing
paint, brushes, shaping hearts like upside down tears,
joined at the base. Some looped with string, clustered
like balloons, bright sacs of breath knotted tight,
as if love could loosen its clutch, this vibrant
sorrow could fade into London's heavy air.

Spring Forward

Twenty-eight wedded years—
pearls slipped from silk thread
knotted in lace. Tonight we set
our clocks forward, and time confounds
us again. Maybe that's why neither
of us can sleep in this Victorian hotel,
floors sinking, mattress slanted,
the baby next door waking to cry.

The years wick away while we
lie here, alert, sifting. I dredge
memory, its dark glints—cannot
recall the name of today's tour guide,
nor the saint in the cathedral's transept,
nor even your mother's presence at our ceremony
though I know she was there. Before our next
pearl is tied she'll wither—with luck
an easeful death untroubled by pain.

Now in midnight's cleft, I'd like
to cradle the wailing baby in my arms,
cup it to my shoulder, hold it there
until the hours of fleeting sleep
dissolve into morning, until I retrieve
what's lost, measure the heft
of each pearl in my palm. Until time swivels
and spring's strand of light is long.

Woodlanders

after Thomas Hardy

You graze the field of my skin,

your finger maps its ridges,
furrows, troughs. No boundary

curbs the longing that roots us

to the earth of one another.
In you I've found my Gabriel Oak

made of thicket and sunlight,

wheat sheaves, harvest,
moon-scythe. You measure the stars,

their cycles, coax spring

lambs, steward seeds,
shore up fences—hearken to

my call across the dusky acres.

Your collarbone cradles my cheek.
Elm twigs brush the windowpane.

Sovereign rivers, we rise,

converge in the woodland,
neither north nor south, shade

nor sunrise, cedar nor oak.

We find each other among trees—
leaf on leaf, skin on skin,

wave upon shoal.

Bodhi

Human brains sprout
like purple cabbage, ample

layers of hearty cupped
leaves. Titmice plunder

retrievers' coats, pluck
gold for the sodding of nests.

Woodpeckers stash seeds
and larvae in shagbarks' cracks,

save for winter bouts
of need. And blue jays learn,

jigger latches, pass
down their tricks to the young.

Knowledge infects hardwoods
too, hub-tree mothers

pulling the others in,
channeling nutrients to saplings,

barking orders through networks
of fungi. All creatures, all plants

want, protect, wither—
suck the sweet sap

of cognizance, strive for the Bodhi,
strain to plant their genes

in the folds of smoldering wombs.
Brilliant with pollen, the backyard

chatters, rattles the garden
gate, glistens with Godhead.

Ghost Fields

On an early drive to Dublin,
black fields of turned soil

exhale whiffs of steam. The mist
collects into sheets, thins to silver

spires. Is this how the body expels
the ghost—pores releasing vapor

into morning haze? Last night
a choir of teenagers sang Rutter's

Gaelic Blessing for the St. Patrick's Day
banquet. The anthem's merging parts

lifted the chapel's rafters, the singers'
airy tones blending with memory,

their voices curling like extravagant coils
of smoke. The closing harmonies twist

and collide, tearing at last through a gate
that opens to meadow and daybreak.

Now countryside streaks past
windowpane, sheaves of steam catch

the shine over fields. Rutter's
discordant strains unravel, settle

into light—clods, tilled ground,
grey-blue sky, fog rising.

IV. Epilogue

Woolsthorpe Manor

Here, while the cattle wander off,
Newton reads in the orchard, studies
apple descent: *What draws the fruit*

keeps the moon from crashing
into the pasture. Inside his cottage
prisms perch on dressers, tables,

plot waves of sun rays—optics,
fragments of white light. Scrawls
on the walls, now faint: Newton's

physics, germinating, sprouting into tree.
The theory is almost right, his numbers
derived from Euclid's limb. But classical

gardens cannot plot a universe,
trace curves in space, the swoop
of time that slides from its axis.

From Newton's tree Einstein
cleaves a scion that twists into sun's
eye, blind as bombs, bends

into Big Bang. And new grafts
from Einstein's branch divide
into strings, quarks, loops of gravity.

What propagates next? Obsolescence?
Inertia? Love? What to do
but claw across the ice, debate

how much a vessel can bear,
if rock and cloud will pull us under
into winter's frigid rush, into drifts—

sleep, the tang of desire, of apple.

Acknowledgments

I am grateful to the following editors for including my work in their publications:

Birmingham Poetry Review: "Marriage at Ten Years, 1963"

Caustic Frolic: "Transfiguration" (pub. as "The Body, Holy Island of Lindesfarne")

Cider Press Review: "Duende"

The Cumberland River Review: "Statistics"

The Dawn Review: "Blue Spruce"

Eunoia Review: "Laid Bare"

Glassworks: "Flight Season"

Hole in the Head Review: "Clutch"

The Inflectionist Review: "Death is not"

Innisfree Poetry Journal: "Octopus"

The Lascaux Review: "Caney Fork"

Minnow Literary Magazine: "Origin Story"(published as "Origin Story, at Fourteen")

Neologism Poetry Journal: "First Language"

One: "After a Long Indiana Winter, 1964"

orangepeel literary magazine: "Ghost Fields"

Passager Journal: "Threadbare"

Plants & Poetry: "Bodhi" (pub. as "The Leafing of Cabbage")

Prometheus Dreaming: "Reverie"

Quartet Journal: "An Ecology of Shells"

Rat's Ass Review: "What the Scan Doesn't Show"

Rockvale Review: "Galloping in Darkness"

Rust & Moth: "Her Offering"

San Pedro River Review: "At sixteen, instead of practicing piano"

Scapegoat Review: "Late"

The Shore: "Portrait of My Father's Glaucoma"

Sky Island Journal: "Keeping Sunrise," "Lava," "Seeds"

SLANT: A Journal of Poetry: "Adagio" (pub. as "End of July")

The Stillwater Review: "Muscle Memory" (pub. as "What Anchors Us")

Stirring: A Literary Collection: "First Morning, 2023"

SWWIM Every Day: "M. Shelley's Interrogation"

Third Wednesday: "Turf"

Valparaiso Poetry Review: "Under a White Moon"

West Trade Review: "Woodlanders"

Whale Road Review: "Spring Forward"

Willawaw Journal: "Daughter, Driving at Night"

Willows Wept Review: "Beyond"

"Memo to a Fledgling," "Our Hands," "Unfolding," and "Woolsthorpe Manor" were published in *The Aeolian Harp*, Vol. 9, eds. Cindy Hochman and Megan Merchant (Glass Lyre Books, 2023).

"On the Brink" was published in *New Feathers Anthology 2023,* eds. Wade Fox, John O'Leary, and Brian Dickson (New Feathers Foundation, 2024).

"At sixteen, instead of practicing piano" was reprinted in *The Last Milkweed Anthology*, ed. Jeffrey Levine (Tupelo Press, 2025).

To Diane Lockward, I am deeply grateful to you for choosing my manuscript and for your belief in this book, as well as for your gracious and incredibly prompt management of the editorial and publishing process. To Gary McDowell, my kind and supportive colleague and friend, thank you for your sharp reading of this manuscript and helpful suggestions. To David Ribar, deep gratitude for the gorgeous cover art— for reading the poems and reinterpreting the book visually. And finally, to my writing groups—Zalon, ZDD, Sunday Poetry, and Moonliters—and especially to my writing partner, Melody Wilson, thank you for your feedback, your encouragement, and most of all, your friendship.

About the Author

Annette Sisson is the author of *Small Fish in High Branches*, published by Glass Lyre (2022). Her poems have been published in *Valparaiso Poetry Review, Birmingham Poetry Review, Rust & Moth, Lascaux Review*, and elsewhere. She won The Porch Writers Collective's 2019 Poetry Prize. She is Professor of English at Belmont University and lives in Nashville, Tennessee.

Printed in the USA
CPSIA information can be obtained
at www.ICGtesting.com
LVHW091914101124
796146LV00001B/10

* 9 7 8 1 9 4 7 8 9 6 7 5 8 *